I'M NOT READY YET

About the pamphlet:
Compulsive overeaters may not want to begin a recovery program because they don't feel "ready." This pamphlet explains why there will never be a better time than now and helps identify some of the attitudes that postpone recovery from eating disorders.

About the author:
Dr. Judi Hollis has been treating addicted families since 1968, and currently specializes in developing hospital eating disorder units, including HOPE Institute (Helping Overeaters thru People and Education). An international lecturer on problems of addiction, she appears regularly on radio and television and is author of the book, *Fat is a Family Affair,* and several pamphlets published by Hazelden Educational Materials. She lives in Hermosa Beach, California.

I'M NOT READY YET

JUDI HOLLIS, Ph.D.

I'M NOT READY YET

I said that I'd leave you anytime I'm ready,
Some April, when all the land is wet.
Some spring, summer, fall, Lord, or maybe winter.
I'll leave some day, but I'm not ready yet . . . .
I knew I shoulda left the day my heart was breakin'
But I broke every date I ever set.
I know I'll leave when my heart tells me it's ready.
But I'm still around 'cause I'm not ready yet.

The country singer wailing this mournful tune knows all too well the struggles of giving up a love gone bad. Despite the harsh reality that the relationship has changed and it won't be the way it was, he hangs around because he's just not ready to leave.

The compulsive overeater's relationship with food is also a love affair gone sour. Even after food is no longer working, even though we're crying while we're bingeing, even with brief periods of control followed by orgies of relief, we still want to believe it can be as it once was. We're sure we can recreate the old relationship. We'll take it back just this once for old times' sake. We'll rely on food to help us make it through the night. Unfortunately, we have to live with the results the next morning and all mornings thereafter.

REASONS I SHOULD NOT START A RECOVERY PROGRAM RIGHT NOW. . . .

Let's take a look at some of the reasons we may not be ready yet.

1. I got engaged.
2. My marriage is splitting up.
3. I don't like my new boss.
4. My best friend moved away.
5. I had a fight with my best friend.
6. My daughter/son started dating.
7. My spouse is working longer hours.

8. I can't get along with/without my children.
9. I will be in/out of the hospital in two weeks.
10. We just bought a freezer.
11. My spouse died.
12. Now I am president of my club.
13. I was promoted to a desk job.
14. We started our own business.
15. I started working part-time.
16. I am/am not pregnant!
17. We've decided to adopt.
18. My spouse wants to have more children.
19. My child is having trouble in school.
20. All my children are/are not in school.
21. My spouse had a heart attack.
22. I've lost interest in sex.
23. My mother is moving in with us.
24. There's a family reunion coming up.
25. We weren't invited.
26. We lost in the stock market.
27. We won the lottery.
28. My daughter got married and they're moving in.
29. We sold the house.
30. My child is starting college.
31. My son entered the army.
32. I'm teaching a new class.
33. My spouse and I are reconciling.
34. I lost my job.
35. I changed jobs.
36. I have too many responsibilities.
37. We are arguing a lot.
38. My spouse is going back to work.
39. I am working nights now.
40. I am traveling too much.
41. I broke my leg.
42. I retired.
43. We're leaving for Europe in two weeks.

44. I am being audited by the IRS.
45. My dog was run over.
46. My cellar was flooded.
47. My kitchen is being remodeled.
48. We were snowbound for two days.
49. We're having a heat wave.
50. I'm in charge of refreshments for the fair.

If any of the preceding statements seems like a reason for you to delay getting started, you're probably not ready yet. There is *always* a "good" reason not to get started. Take two weeks of vacation a year, then add all the birthdays of near and distant relatives, throw in all the long weekends with Monday holidays, add in the two-month binge between Halloween and New Year's Day, anniversaries, parties, and ordinary entertaining, and the total will be 267 days per year that are bad for start-up!

All the holidays and all the reasonable excuses don't really justify keeping ourselves miserable. They are merely rationalizations that will keep us sick. When we realize compulsive eating is an illness, these excuses cannot so easily be rationalized. It's never convenient; there will never be a better time than now! If you had cancer, would you cancel a chemotherapy appointment because you had to wait for the gardener? Would you explain that your treatments would have to wait until after the holidays?

WHO NEEDS THIS MESS?

"Well, I certainly don't need more bad news!" you explode. "It's a dirty deal and a rotten shame, and I want no part of this!" Well, no one ever said we would like it. We just have to accept that the program of Overeaters Anonymous works and our own ways don't. In fact, if you think about it, "our ways" have brought us to where we are now. If the old ways worked, we'd be reading the funny papers instead of searching for more answers. Our present condition is certainly not due to lack of effort. Instead, it is misdirected energy. We really believe we're not hurting enough to need help. *We're saying, "I can do it myself."*

In truth, we're not ever going to feel any more ready for help than we do now. If we don't start in the midst of our present turmoil, we'll never get started at all. For a time, we may need to think of O.A. meetings as medicine prescribed to heal this illness. Not all medicines taste good. Some that taste sweeter aren't as effective as others. Just like any other illness, it is best to follow the prescription even if we don't feel like it right now. O.A. suggests, "Take the body and the mind will follow." It's okay to wail, "Please ma, I don't wanna go." We don't have to wanna. A newcomer once asked an old-timer, "How long do I have to go to meetings?" The reply was, "You have to go until you *want* to go. Then you won't *have to* anymore."

The Twelve Step recovery program promises we will have to work at it for a lifetime. We may prefer to go many rounds with shots, pills, gyms, or fad diets, always hoping we can put out some effort for awhile, be successful, and be done with it. The O.A. program suggests instead that our whole lifestyle must change, and change will continue from now until we die.

When we are getting ready to truly accept recovery, we instinctively know nothing tastes as good as abstinence feels. No matter what, how, where, when, or with whom we eat, our relationship with food just isn't the same anymore. If we can't believe this is true, we should go back and try all our old favorites just one more time. Unfortunately, we just wouldn't get what we needed. The love affair is over. *What used to solve our problems has become the problem.* Many people face this painful reality and then respond to crisis, pain, discomfort, or nausea the same way they always have: they *eat*.

A SIMPLE PROGRAM FOR COMPLICATED PEOPLE

The O.A. prescription suggests avoiding the paralysis of analysis. *Action* is the magic word. We must become ready to change our whole lives. Simple project? Not at all. However, our readiness is absolutely necessary. We can't live the same life, continue the same behaviors, and not expect the same consequences.

Getting ready requires very little intellectual effort, but does call for a tremendous amount of common sense. Old-timers in O.A. promise, "There are none too dumb for this Program, but some are too smart." We have to give up searching for intellectual answers or justifying why the Program does or doesn't work. In this case, our compulsive-obsessive eating has kept us preoccupied, and we've been out of contact with our real selves. We've deprived ourselves of a life of peace and contentment guided by a *still, small voice within*. We cannot stay in conscious contact with our spirituality if we are busy justifying and explaining our behavior.

A spiritual awakening is necessary; we must come to believe there is something better. We will find our abstinence evolves from our right living. When we are rigorously honest with ourselves, we will achieve rightness of body. We can't think ourselves into right living, but we can live ourselves into right thinking.

If we seek guidance from our minds, rather than our spirits, we trap ourselves in self-justification and rationalization. Our minds will guard our egos at the expense of the inner selves we choose to disown. When we behave in new ways, even in ways foreign to our egos now, the gates to our souls will open.

DON'T TRY TO FIGURE IT OUT

Those of us who have had therapy and more history exploring personal insights usually have more difficulty accepting a spiritual recovery. We may have been taught to seek answers, not take action. Knowing all the reasons *why* we eat will do very little to help us stop eating. Actually, if we were to uncover some of the reasons, we might feel so depressed we'd eat! Insight is a booby prize. If knowing *why* helped, we wouldn't be here now.

Wayne had spent many years in therapy before attending his first O.A. meeting. At that first meeting he sat in the back row and judged what everyone said. "My God, they are operating on such a superficial level. Why, I worked through these issues my very first year in therapy. What can I possibly learn from these amateurs?" Despite whatever separated him from the others, Wayne knew there was one thing they had in common: "These people know the pain I'm in. They know about those midnight raids on the refrigerator, and they know how out of control I feel. They know how hard it is to ask for a separate chair at a restaurant because I can't fit into a booth! They also, oddly enough, seem to know how to stay thin."

Wayne decided to stay, find a sponsor, and start working the O.A. program. He didn't know yet that these members had a tremendous gift to share with him. They were taking on the journey of self-discovery while abstinent. They were taking on new behaviors and their lives were changing. These people believed they wouldn't be given more than they could handle. They knew that wherever they were and whatever they were doing was right for now. This assurance came from a faith in the rightness of abstinence. These people were open and their feelings were raw without the option of seeking solace in food. Their simple credo was, "Don't eat compulsively, no matter what happens."

After two weeks of healthy, guilt-free eating, and daily talks with his sponsor, Wayne was feeling great. He was now calm and confident. Suddenly, for no apparent reason, he found himself in a donut shop buying a dozen donuts, and bingeing in his van all the way home. Shocked and appalled, he called his sponsor to explain what had happened. "I'm sure it must be due to the pressures at work. I'm just too overworked. Or maybe it's because my mom is coming out to visit. You know I get nervous around her. Or, I bet it's because I'm losing weight and I'm really afraid to get thin. Or quite possibly I'm fearful about my sexuality and don't want to be thin and attractive. Maybe it could be boredom. I don't know how to have fun without food."

The list continued, and when Wayne had finished, his sponsor offered the following. "Wayne, you binged because you are a compulsive overeater. We eat because our team wins or because it loses. Your natural state is to be bingeing and, by working the Steps of this Program, you are offered a daily spiritual reprieve. Sometimes the illness strikes despite all our best efforts. You will not be able to control it by learning to understand it."

Thinking surely his sponsor couldn't really believe this, Wayne responded, "How can we expect to recover if we can't figure it out?" The answer is we can't; abstinence is a reprieve, not a cure. This event set Wayne on a whole new path, as he began trusting in the possibility of spiritual healing for a physical affliction. As Wayne slowly gave up his analyzing, he began to ask his sponsor questions about his life instead of about his food. He learned he had no control over his affliction and needed to call others in the Program when the demon hit. The only safety was in turning to others and leaving his intellect behind. Wayne quipped to a newcomer, "I'm amazed at how smart I was when I got here, and how much I had to forget in order to begin recovering. Funny, I don't feel the loss. Except for the weight, that is."

Sometimes doctors, nurses, and other health care professionals suffer most with the intellectual approach to this illness. Their profession is *based* on controlling illness through the power of reason. This gives them feelings of worth and power. Sometimes it is excruciatingly painful for them to accept that they have to give up control in order to recover. They find it very difficult to share with other O.A.s individually and at meetings. They believe it would be unprofessional for them to air their dirty linen around others. Some feel it would be detrimental for others to see their human frailties. Perhaps they even fear damage to their self-images, thinking a professional *should* have all the answers. They, too, must learn the road to recovery involves facing their human neediness and fallibility.

KEEP IT SIMPLE

We still may not be ready to give up our rational approach to recovery. After all, our answers did work for brief periods of time. We probably judge ourselves harshly, assuming it is our fault if those answers stopped working. "I certainly learned in behavior modification class how to put down my fork between bites. If I would have continued doing that, I'd be thin by now." It's easy to miss the simple fact that we need help daily to practice and remember simple things we already know. While our personal blinders can make us forgetful, a caring person who knows the ways we deceive ourselves can help us stay motivated and committed.

Simple instructions help us take active measures that bring success. The commitment to *utilize, not analyze* is illustrated in the following "shaggy tire" story.

A very sane, reasonable, well-dressed man finds himself driving alongside the chain link fence securing the grounds to the state mental hospital, when his car lurches forward with a blowout. Upon investigation, he finds that the wheel has come off because all four lugnuts have fallen off. Having a useable spare, he still has no idea how to replace the tire without lugnuts. A patient hangs onto the fence observing this dilemma. Seeing the motorist's pain and confusion, the patient offers, "Why don't you take one nut off each of the other three wheels so that each have three, and you can get into town to get your new ones later?"

"Brilliant!" responds the motorist and sets to the job at hand. Before driving off, he thanks the patient with, "You are a very bright guy. Why are you on that side of the fence?"

The patient smiles broadly, "I may be crazy, but I'm not stupid!"

IT'S A QUESTION OF BALANCE

A successful recovery will require the same amount of energy and commitment that bingeing once did. All the time and energy formerly devoted to planning, discussing, and finally executing binges must now be redirected toward abstinence and serenity. Oddly enough, many shy away from this by complaining, "I'm too weak, too sick. Wait 'til I'm more ready." We never complained we were too sick for just one more bite. We were *always* ready to eat.

Often other people are the reasons we use for not caring for ourselves. Notice how many of the reasons listed earlier had to do with other people. Either someone else is keeping us from taking care of ourselves, or others' needs come first. We think it is gracious to keep our promises to others, but selfish to keep promises to ourselves. Daily contact with a sponsor is important, because our tendency to keep our promises to others may cause us to forget our commitments to ourselves.

As human beings, we are given the freedom to choose. We are given tremendous responsibility for our lives. We are facing decisions about our expenditure of energy: where and how we choose to invest the precious moments of our lives. Every instant dominated by food or thoughts of food is a stolen breath of life.

In Viktor Frankl's book, *Man's Search For Meaning*, episodes of such decisive moments are chronicled. He and fellow prisoners had to make choices as they endured domination in Nazi concentration camps. Some prisoners were seeking power in a powerless situation and took on many of the behaviors of their guards. They emulated a negative power source. Others were able to maintain their integrity and sense of values despite whatever torture was visited upon them. Frankl concluded that we all have choices about the stimuli we respond to, and therefore, we can all make decisions about the quality of our lives.

In this light, the spiritual aspect of recovery becomes more important to us. Once we have chosen a spiritual course, we are assured that no one can take our souls away. While we are compulsively eating, we participate in whittling our souls and integrity away. Choosing to stay obsessed with food is choosing to turn over possibilities of a good life to others more ready.

ARE WE CHOOSING TO BE SICK?

Notice how many overeaters are also plagued by physical maladies. Certainly they suffer complications produced by their excess weight. Disease and germs are circulating all the time, but perhaps these people have chosen to be sick. These people wouldn't complain when a medical appointment scheduled for 2:00 P.M. doesn't begin until 4:00. They would believe the doctor's time is more valuable than their own. But it's not just an afternoon, it's their lives they waste this way. Those patients might answer, "But I'm sick, what do you want me to do?" That lament may be true. Waiting passively is one of the necessary evils of being a sick person.

The deeper matter to consider is the decision to be a sick person. Will you be one? How about choosing to take a bike ride at the beach instead? Many people in recovery complain it is hard to learn how to have a good time. Who knows how to ride a bike? It is a matter of choice. Some people choose that ride over sitting in a doctor's waiting room. Should the doctor go to Puerto Rico or should it be your trip? Did you admire the Mercedes your dentist bought? You helped pay for it with the braces and caps you needed after all the vomiting episodes rotted your teeth. Why should we use destructive ways to cope with our lives while those who clean up after our destruction make their choices to relax on the beach or take leisurely drives in the sun?

Alexis has been through three different hospital treatment programs and two long-term stints in analysis. Last year alone, her father spent $40,000 on her medical bills. Thus far, her self-destruction has cost $69,000! She has chosen to spend her inheritance through medical claim forms.

DOES THE DEVIL MAKE US DO IT?

The same person who drives a full hour to try a newly opened restaurant will complain that O.A. meetings are too far away. Despite whatever "gung ho" willingness they had upon first entering recovery, many start to balk around the third or fourth day. When withdrawals are influencing us, it seems very reasonable to stop doing what we've started. "It's not working. It's been three days already!" How many second chances and special considerations have we given to food? When we tasted something that seemed a little off, maybe moldy or sour, didn't we take just another little taste to make sure? Weren't we hoping the initial turn-off would change to a turn-on? We have to be willing to give O.A. the same second chances we give to food.

Some days the demon wakes up a half hour earlier than we do. He can be sitting at the edge of the bed devising elaborate schemes to convince us to give up: "Look at this cloudy day! Who could start something new on a cloudy day? We're going to a wedding this Sunday anyway. Here it is Thursday; we started this thing on Monday and we're into heavy withdrawals by now. Let's give it up and start again next Monday. Who diets on the weekends anyway?" Before we've rubbed the sleep from our eyes, this grand debate sets up the day even before we're out of bed. We will need to mobilize an

11

even bigger investment of energy toward recovery to counteract this natural state of wanting food. It is much easier to maintain the status quo than to initiate new behavior. As compulsive overeaters, our natural state is bingeing. Our great tendency is to choose this "natural" behavior. After all, we've been living this way for a long time.

Nancy found how cunning, baffling, powerful, and patient this demon was when she observed herself change direction so quickly that she said it was like an out-of-body experience. Despite her strong motivation and drive toward recovery, she talked herself back into bingeing in half an hour. She contacted our treatment center desperately out of control. She said she'd do anything to get help for herself right away. She lived in Canada, and when she called she was not sure she could make the trip. When the staff informed her we could admit her right away and someone would pick her up at the airport, she was suddenly no longer ready. She had to get certain affairs in order. She had financial problems. She needed someone to care for her cats, was afraid of airplanes, was scheduled for job interviews, was planning her sister's birthday, her brother needed her support through final exams, etc. She set an admission date three weeks away.

Within three days she called back and said she was ready. Her "affairs" were actually the need to keep eating. However, once she had set a date for starting a new way of life, the bingeing became boring even as she continued to eat. She was more excited about starting recovery than in reliving the old tried and true disappointment with food. She was ready.

Three weeks into Nancy's treatment, the newness and fun had worn off and the hard work of recovery and facing herself was at hand. It took much less than three days to convince her to run back. She was irritated and scared about the self-examination that surfaced when she didn't have food for solace. She was judgmental and intolerant of staff and other patients, but rather than express those feelings, she went undergound and began planning her departure. The demon

12

convinced her, "they" had made her do it. Confronting "them" with her true and honest feelings would have been an investment in her own recovery. Instead, one night at 2:00 A.M., Nancy packed her bags and flew home. She had stopped at a deli on her way to the airport and the taxi was strewn with cellophane wrappers.

The minute her plane landed in Toronto, she telephoned, sobbing, "How could I have made such a mistake and executed it so quickly? I'm standing here in the middle of Canada and feel like I've had a blackout. How did I get here?" Nancy got there by carefully avoiding being honest with others about her true feelings. Since she felt guilty about what she was feeling, she let her resentments eventually walk her away from recovery. She traded abstinence for the "nice girl" image she wanted to protect. She was so shocked at her ability to give it all up so quickly that she immediately returned to bingeing. When the obsession to eat takes over, there are few obstacles that can keep us from food. When our obsession is running rampant, life is chaotic. Nancy was bewildered to see that getting to treatment required elaborate planning and thoughtful consideration, while running *from* treatment occurred on a momentary whim. In an unthinking instant each of us can reverse self-healing into self-destruction. Intelligence or motivation has nothing to do with it. Nancy's resourcefulness could match anyone's as she got herself to the airport, reserved a flight, and bought her "stash" for the trip home. That unwitting, powerful energy is awesome when it is directed toward self-abuse.

TIMING BATTLES WITH GOD

Many of us avoid change by getting into timing battles with God. "It's not time. I don't feel comfortable. It doesn't seem the most *reasonable* course of action. I've got to think about it some more."

Edward fought out a dramatic timing battle with God. He lived in a rough neighborhood and was clearly getting signals that he had to move. He talked about this at meetings for weeks. "It's getting dangerous. There were three robberies and muggings just last week. I just don't seem to find the time to look for a new place. I guess I will when I'm good and ready." Edward was found beaten to death in his apartment. Time had run out. He was trading willingness for wishfulness and, though he talked well, he was not ready to follow through with action. Hopefully, delays won't be as deadly for us.

WHAT GOES AROUND COMES AROUND

Sidney was a successful businessman with two years in the Program. He had lost over 100 pounds and still had about 50 to go. He felt good about his recovery and himself, and by all standards he was a success in the world. He was doing well, but he didn't like others who weren't. One night he was asked to speak at a special O.A. meeting. Sidney liked speaking at O.A. as it gave him a chance to hear his own echo. Instead of focusing on business, he could focus on himself. Listening to himself talk helped him learn who he really was. On this particular night he learned about his own power to create his destiny.

Sidney's sponsor had taught him, "Bloom where you are planted" and "Be here now." He was instructed to speak about whatever popped into his mind rather than rehearse a canned pitch to impress or wow the folks. Sidney left his management style at the office; O.A. was his forum for spontaneity. He began his talk by recounting the events of his harried business day. He was agitated by a clerk he felt was a "flake."

"I just can't stand people who are always needy and make others responsible for them. They are always asking for favors or wanting others to bail them out. It's always some jam or crisis *they* create and then they impose the results on the rest of us to fix." Ultimately, Sidney's talk focused on "responsibility" and avoiding people who expect too much. He was very hot that night about "irresponsible, demanding, immature" people. His judgments were out in full bloom.

After the meeting, he returned to his car where his judgments came home to roost. His car had been towed! Sidney stomped his foot as he remembered seeing the no parking sign, figuring it didn't apply to him. "I can get away with it just this once," he had said to himself. He hurried back to find some people from the meeting clearing tables. He sheepishly asked for a ride to the towing yard. Embarrassed and humiliated at the self-inflicted jam, he was forced to ask for help. When he paid the fine and recovered his car, he casually asked what time the towing occurred. "Eight-thirty," responded the attendant, precisely the moment that Sidney had started his tirade about "flakes." Consequences were appearing simultaneously with his judgments. In simple terms, "What goes around comes around." We need to be careful about what we say and what we do.

ARE YOU READY YET?

If not now, when? There is really no option about *whether* to jump into a full-fledged recovery or not. The question is *when?* This illness is progressive; it always gets worse, never better. Our intolerance to food abuse progresses outside our awareness and will continue whether we are bingeing or not. Just as with any other love affair, we can't go back to how it used to be.

Sometimes we delay taking action, thinking we can avoid the consequences. This is rarely the case because the universe continues and our lives will unfold whether we decide to actively participate or not. Not making a decision is, in itself, a decision. If we have made no decision, we have decided to remain passive and take what comes. There is no escape from life, just as there is no free lunch.

We must be ready to say, "I might as well face my life because food is no longer working." When we are abstinent from compulsive eating, our bodies will give us clear signals about what behaviors we can or cannot tolerate. When our recovery follows a spiritual path, we will gain clearer vision and more readily see the relationship between events in our lives and our own intentions and decisions. We will be ready to listen to the wisdom of that "still, small voice within." Though messages may reveal lifestyle changes we don't feel ready for yet, we may have to proceed, ready or not. *Are you ready?*

Hazelden

Other titles that will interest you...

Fat Is a Family Affair
by Judi Hollis, Ph.D.

Fat Is a Family Affair describes how recovery from an eating disorder requires a journey to find the real self. Written directly to eating disorder sufferers and those who love them, *Fat Is a Family Affair* is a complete discussion of the disease and the family's involvement. It gives specific guidance for learning how to express our needs, turn to other people for help, and confront the world with who we really are. (180 pp.)
Order No. 1091A

Accepting Powerlessness
by Judi Hollis, Ph.D.

Another look at Step One for overeaters, Kubler-Ross' five stages of dying are applied to several types and examples of denial. The author says we face one basic issue: "Can we accept having a lifelong, terminal illness which will require intense treatment if it is to become manageable?" (32 pp.)
Order No. 1221B

Relapse for Eating Disorder Sufferers
by Judi Hollis, Ph.D.

This pamphlet is a thorough discussion of how to anticipate and guard against relapse to compulsive eating habits. We are taught to recognize the major signs of relapse: hunger, anger, loneliness, and tiredness, and cautioned that learning to be honest with ourselves, and adherence to our own internal standards, are the all-important lessons for staying abstinent. (28 pp.)
Order No. 1392B

**For price and order information, please call one of our
Customer Service Representatives.**

Hazelden
Educational Materials

Pleasant Valley Road
Box 176
Center City, MN 55012-0176

(800) 328-9000
(Toll Free. U.S. Only)
(800) 257-0070
(Toll Free. MN Only)
(800) 328-0500
(Toll Free. Film and Video
Orders. U.S. Only)
(612) 257-4010
(Alaska and Outside U.S.)

Order No. 5356   ISBN: 0-89486-372-X